CONTENTS

Words in **bold** can be found in the glossary on page 30.

The history detective Sherlock Bones will help you to find clues and collect evidence about early Islamic civilization. Wherever you see one of Sherlock's paw-prints, you will find a mystery to solve. The answers are on page 31.

HOW DID ISLAM START?

From the seventh to the thirteenth centuries CE, the Islamic Empire controlled vast stretches of Asia, Africa and Europe. Its extraordinary leaders, soldiers, scholars and scientists made the empire one of the most advanced civilizations the world had ever seen. The story of Islamic civilization starts with the birth of the Prophet Muhammad ﷺ.

Muhammad ﷺ was born in the city of Mecca in around 570 CE. Mecca was in a region called Arabia, in western Asia. The people who lived in Arabia spoke a language called **Arabic** and are often called Arabs. At this time, there were many different tribes in Arabia. Most Arabs were **pagans**, but a few tribes were Christian or Jewish.

Muhammad ﷺ often went to pray in a cave in the mountains outside Mecca. It was here that, in around 610 CE, Muhammad ﷺ reported he had received his first **revelation** from God. He began to preach that there is one God. This was the birth of the religion called Islam, which means 'surrender to God'. Believers are called Muslims. The holy book of Islam is the Quran. Muslims believe that it contains the words of God, as revealed to the Prophet Muhammad ﷺ.

DETECTIVE WORK

Find out more about the life of Muhammad ﷺ and the teachings of Islam at: http://www.islamkids.org.

This copy of the Quran was handwritten, using ink and gold leaf, in Arabic. It was made in Egypt during the ninth or tenth century. For early Muslims, the Quran was essential for spreading the word of Islam.

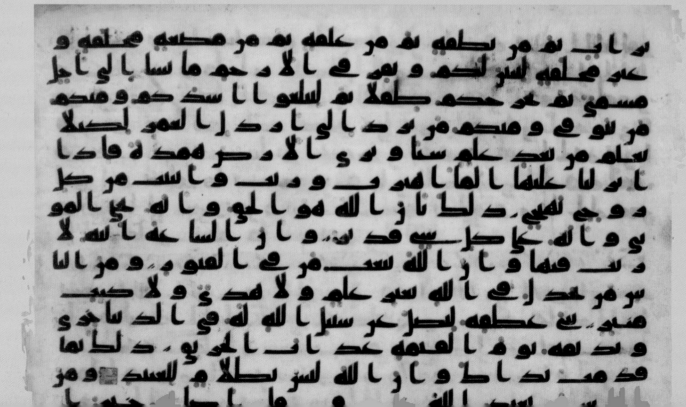

In 622 CE, hostility from the leading families in Mecca made Muhammad ﷺ and his followers move to Medina, 330 km (200 miles) to the north. Here they founded a Muslim community. The Islamic calendar counts years from this event, known as the Hijra. The first year of the calendar is 622 CE, known as 1 AH (from the Latin *anno Hegirae*, 'in the year of the Hijra'). From Medina, Muhammad ﷺ and his followers spread the word of Islam across Arabia. When they met with opposition from hostile tribes, the growing Muslim army waged war against them. In 632 CE, Muhammad ﷺ fell ill and died. He had succeeded in uniting many of the tribes of Arabia, and **converting** most Arabs to Islam.

Now Muhammad's ﷺ followers needed to select a new leader for the Muslim people. They chose Abu Bakr, who was Muhammad's ﷺ father-in-law and close friend. As Muhammad's ﷺ successor, he was named 'caliph', which comes from the Arabic *khalifa*, meaning 'someone who comes after'. Under Abu Bakr's rule, the Muslim army began to attack the Byzantine **Empire** and the Sassanid Empire, whose lands lay just to the north of Arabia. As they conquered lands outside Arabia, the first caliphs started to build their own empire. The spread of Islamic civilization had begun.

The Dome of the Rock mosque in Jerusalem was completed in 691 CE. Mosques are where Muslims can pray, meet and study.

In his last sermon, in 632 CE, Muhammad ﷺ said:

'O People, lend me an attentive ear, for I don't know whether, after this year, I shall ever be amongst you again. Therefore listen to what I am saying to you carefully and take these words to those who could not be present here today.'

What symbol is on top of the Dome of the Rock's dome?

HOW BIG WAS THE ISLAMIC EMPIRE?

The Islamic Empire had reached its greatest size by the 730s CE. In 100 years, Muslim armies had conquered 15 million square kilometres (5.8 million sq miles) – around 10 per cent of the Earth's land area. Nearly one third of the world's population was ruled by the caliphs.

The rule of the first four caliphs after the death of Muhammad ﷺ is known as the Rashidun **caliphate**. Rashidun comes from the Arabic for 'rightly guided', because these men had been close companions of Muhammad ﷺ. The armies of the Rashidun caliphs extended Islamic rule throughout Arabia and began to push outwards into western Asia and eastern North Africa.

In 661 CE, the last of the Rashidun caliphs, Ali, was attacked by a **rebel** and died from his wounds. One of the Muslim army's most powerful generals, Muawiyah, declared himself caliph. Muawiyah was a member of the **Umayyad** family, who came from Mecca, and he was the first caliph of the Umayyad **dynasty**. During the rule of the Umayyads, the empire grew to its greatest size: it stretched across North Africa and the **Middle East** as far as modern Pakistan. In Europe, most of the Iberian Peninsula (modern Spain and Portugal) fell under the caliphs' control.

DETECTIVE WORK

Chart the growth of the Islamic Empire using this interactive map: http://www.vam.ac.uk/vastatic/microsites/1342_islamic_middle_east/map/.

This map shows the growth of the Islamic Empire from the death of Muhammad ﷺ to its largest size.

RUSSIA
EUROPE
FRANCE
SPAIN
CORDOBA GRANADA
TURKEY
SAMARKAND
ASIA
CHINA
MOROCCO
SYRIA IRAQ IRAN
DAMASCUS BAGHDAD
CAIRO
DELHI
EGYPT
MEDINA
MECCA
SAUDI ARABIA
INDIA
AFRICA
INDIAN OCEAN

1000 KM
1000 MILES

ATLANTIC OCEAN

☐ ISLAMIC CALIPHATE BY 632
☐ ISLAMIC CALIPHATE BY 661
☐ ISLAMIC CALIPHATE BY 750

COUNTRIES ARE LABELLED WITH THEIR MODERN NAMES

In 750 CE, the Umayyads were overthrown by another family from Mecca, the **Abbasids**. The Abbasids were deeply influenced by the Quran's teachings about the importance of education, charity and good government. During the Abbasid caliphate, Islamic civilization moved into what historians call its **golden age**.

While some **provinces** of the empire were closely controlled, others were quite independent, as long as they paid their **taxes**. In some regions, there were constant rebellions. By 945 CE, the Abbasid caliphate had lost control of nearly all its provinces. These areas were still under Muslim power, but were ruled by many separate leaders. The Abbasid caliphs remained figureheads but they no longer had authority over their empire. The Abbasid caliphate formally came to an end in 1258 CE, when the last caliph, al-Musta'sim, was overthrown. Although this was the end of a golden age, it was not the end for Islamic civilization. By 1500 CE, Islamic rule had extended to India, Turkey and much of north and central Africa.

Umar (584/9–644 CE), the second Rashidun caliph, told his governors:

'*Remember, I have not appointed you as commanders and tyrants over the people. I have sent you as leaders instead, so that the people may follow your example.*'

What was the purpose of a minaret?

Construction started on this 72-m (238-ft) minaret, called the Qutb Minar, in 1199 CE. It was part of the first mosque built in Delhi after the Islamic conquest of India.

WHAT WEAPONS DID ISLAMIC WARRIORS USE?

The army that spread Islamic civilization was large, organized and well disciplined. The troops were under the command of generals, who were appointed by the caliph. Soldiers used swords, spears and bows.

In 632 CE, the year of Muhammad's ﷺ death, the Islamic army numbered just 13,000 men. By the time the Umayyads came to power in 661 CE, the caliph could raise an army of up to 100,000 men. In comparison, the largest European armies of the time hardly ever numbered more than 7,000 men. The Umayyads succeeded in making most of the army professional, which means that the soldiers were paid a salary for working full time. Their salaries came from taxes paid to the caliphate. The Umayyads also created a strong **navy** to support the army from the sea.

DETECTIVE WORK

To do some research of your own about the ways in which Islamic arms and armour have developed through history, have a look at the collection at the Metropolitan Museum of Art, in New York: http://www.metmuseum.org/toah/hd/isaa/hd_isaa.htm.

This bust of an Umayyad soldier (shown here reflected in a mirror so you can see two views of it) was made in around 700 CE. He is wearing an egg-shaped helmet of iron or bronze.

In the early years, most of the Islamic army fought on foot, although they often travelled to the battlefield on horses or camels. These foot soldiers, known as infantry, were armed with spears, swords and bows and arrows. The spears, made from reeds, were up to 2.5 m (8 ft) long. They were mostly used for thrusting at the enemy rather than throwing. The Islamic sword was called a *sayf*. Soldiers also carried a dagger, which was kept as a last resort. Their wooden bows had a firing range of up to 150 m (490 ft). Over time, specialist divisions of skilled archers, known as the *rumat*, were established.

At the start of a battle, when the enemies were a distance apart, the Islamic archers fired their arrows. When the enemies had drawn close, there was hand-to-hand combat with swords and spears. A few soldiers, known as the cavalry, were mounted on horses or camels during battle. These cavalrymen were armed with lances (strong spears) and swords. Their leather or **chainmail** armour was lighter than the infantry's, so their animals could move fast.

In this tenth- to twelfth-century Egyptian illustration, cavalrymen are fighting fiercely with lances.

🐾 **What did the cavalry use lances for?**

For at least the first 100 years of the Islamic army, the cavalry was used just for **skirmishes** in battle, relying on speed to make sudden attacks to the backs and sides of the enemy ranks. The cavalry was also useful for carrying messages. They did not often use bows, because riders were open to attack when they had to stop and fire. But from the early ninth century, Turkish soldiers were recruited to the Islamic army. These men could fire on the gallop. In the open landscapes of the Middle East, these swiftly moving horse archers were dangerous. As time went on, the Islamic army relied more and more on its cavalry.

In around 632 CE, the army general 'Amr ibn al-'As spoke about the skills of another great general, Khalid ibn al-Walid:

'He is a master of war; a friend of death. He has the dash of a lion and the patience of a cat!'

WAS EVERYONE IN THE EMPIRE A MUSLIM?

The armies of the Umayyad caliphate extended the empire very quickly, so quickly that the spread of Islam was slow to catch up. In 750 CE, only around 8 out of every 100 residents in the empire were Muslim. Muslims were still a minority in the empire until the tenth century. As long as everyone paid taxes to the caliph, they could live in the empire, whatever their religion.

When Muslim armies conquered a new region, the people they met were often pagans, Christians, Jews or **Zoroastrians**. Over time, many of the non-Muslims living in the empire converted to Islam, but they were not usually forced to. Throughout the golden age of Islamic civilization, some respected scholars and officials were not Muslims. However, people who did not convert to Islam usually had to pay higher taxes and had fewer legal rights than Muslims.

Islam was the heart of the caliphate. The caliph ruled in the name of God and Islam. Everyone had to obey Muslim law, called *Shari'a*, whatever their religion. Shari'a covered all areas of people's public and private lives: debts, wills, business partnerships, marriage and slavery, along with prayer, fasting and charity.

The Abbasid caliph al-Mutawakkil was a keen builder. In 848 CE, he ordered the construction of the spiralling Malwiya (meaning 'snail shell') minaret, in Samarra (modern Iraq). It formed part of what was then the largest mosque in the world.

The Abbasid judge and scholar Ibn Qutaybah (828–889 CE) wrote:

'There can be no government without an army,
No army without money,
No money without prosperity,
And no prosperity without justice and good administration.'

Public life in the empire was centred on Islam and the mosque. As well as being places for prayer, mosques were meeting points, where important announcements were made. The Umayyad caliphs themselves led Friday prayers in their central mosque. Nearly everyone observed Muslim religious holidays, such as **Ramadan**. On the date of Muhammad's ﷺ birthday, officials made speeches and there were feasts.

Muslim women were not supposed to be seen regularly in public, so family life was centred on the home, for people of all religions. The homes of wealthier people were built around airy courtyards, where they might play chess or backgammon, sing, tell stories or recite poetry. Poorer people lived in simpler, flat-roofed houses, made of mud. Women from poorer families often had more freedom outside their homes, as they had no choice but to work as farmers or animal herders.

DETECTIVE WORK

Find out more about mosques and Islamic art from all over the world on this website: http://www.discoverislamicart.org/index.php.

This thirteenth-century illustration shows pilgrims travelling to Mecca. Pilgrimage to Mecca, called Hajj, is a duty for all able-bodied Muslims at least once during their life.

The Umayyad mosque in Damascus (modern Syria) was completed by 715 CE. Its courtyard is paved with marble and surrounded by arcades.

Why did early mosques (and many mosques today) have courtyards?

WHERE WAS THE 'ROUND CITY'?

During the first centuries after it was founded, Baghdad (in modern Iraq) was often known as the 'round city' because it was designed on a circular plan. The construction of the city was ordered in 762 CE by Caliph al-Mansur (714–775 CE), who intended it to be the capital for the new Abbasid caliphate.

It was usual for new dynasties to build new capitals to signal a fresh start. Al-Mansur was the second caliph of the Abbasid caliphate, which had overthrown the previous Umayyad caliphate in 750 CE. The Umayyads' capital had been Damascus (in modern Syria). Al-Mansur and his advisers chose the site of his new city carefully, in fertile countryside and on important trade routes.

It took four years and the efforts of over 100,000 workers to build the round city. Construction started in July 764 CE, as **astrologers** had suggested that the city's foundations be laid under the zodiac sign of Leo. Leo represented growth. The city was surrounded by two thick walls, 30 m (98 ft) high, and a water-filled moat. The four iron entry gates were so heavy that it took six men to open them. The city's walls and buildings were constructed from brick, with plentiful use of marble.

DETECTIVE WORK

To discover more about the history of Baghdad, have a look at this website: http://www.whyislam.org/muslim-world/baghdad-3/.

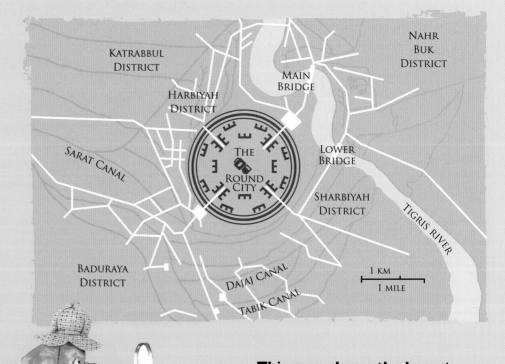

KATRABBUL DISTRICT

NAHR BUK DISTRICT

HARBIYAH DISTRICT

MAIN BRIDGE

SARAT CANAL

THE ROUND CITY

LOWER BRIDGE

SHARBIYAH DISTRICT

TIGRIS RIVER

BADURAYA DISTRICT

DAJAJ CANAL

TABIK CANAL

1 KM

1 MILE

This map shows the layout of Baghdad in the ninth century. The central round city is surrounded by numerous suburbs, as well as roads and canals.

🐾 What natural feature was key to Baghdad's success?

The round city's design was intended to **symbolize** both the Earth and the heavens. The circle was divided into quarters by two grand avenues. At the centre was the caliph's palace, along with the Great Mosque. From this central point, the caliph symbolically ruled over not just the four quarters of the world, but also over the powers of chaos in the universe.

Baghdad soon grew far outside the original circular walls. Business people, scholars, workers, Muslims, Christians, Jews and pagans all flocked to the capital. By the tenth century, Baghdad had over a million inhabitants, making it the largest city in the world. Outside the central round city were countless homes, mosques, libraries and schools, as well as gardens, racecourses, concert halls, gambling houses and theatres. In the busy streets and markets, poorer people were entertained by storytellers, shadow theatre shows, and cock- and ram-fighting.

By the thirteenth century, the power of the Abbasids and their capital had waned. In 1258 CE, Baghdad was captured by Mongols from central Asia. They killed many of the city's inhabitants, burnt its libraries, and destroyed most of its buildings and monuments. The city's – and the empire's – golden age had come to an end.

Within just a few years of Baghdad's construction, palaces, mosques and homes had covered both banks of the River Tigris.

Al-Masudi (896–956 CE) was a historian born in Baghdad. He wrote:

'In Baghdad, there was a street storyteller who amused the crowd with all sorts of tales and funny stories. His name was Ibn Maghazili… As he told his stories, he added many jokes which would have made a mourning mother laugh and would have amused a serious man.'

In these fourteenth-century Persian paintings, the Mongol army is seen besieging Baghdad in 1258 CE. Defenders are firing arrows from the city walls.

WHAT COULD YOU BUY IN BAGHDAD'S MARKETS?

The markets and shops of Baghdad were filled with foods and crafts from across the empire and beyond. The side streets around the bustling, noisy shopping districts were lined with the warehouses of merchants and the workshops of craftspeople.

The caliphs spent money on improving **irrigation** across the empire, bringing a steadier supply of water to their hot, at times desert, lands. Waterwheels were often used to lift water from rivers into canals, which carried water to the fields and cities. Before the days of good irrigation, people in the Middle East ate a simple diet, with lots of barley and dates (which needed little water to grow) along with milk and cheese. But Baghdad's markets were stocked with a wider range of foods, particularly fruits and grains. Wealthy people might eat rich meat stews, flavoured with pomegranate or cheese, and herbs and spices. Puddings and biscuits, sweetened with almonds or syrup, were popular.

Made in the twelfth or thirteenth century, this ceramic bottle is in the shape of a musician playing an *oud*. Traces of gold paint can still be seen.

DETECTIVE WORK

Choose your favourite object from among the British Museum's collection of Islamic craftwork: http://www. britishmuseum.org/ explore/cultures/ middle_east/islamic_ middle_east.aspx.

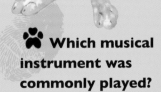

Which musical instrument was commonly played?

As Baghdad grew, merchants from all over the Middle East came to the city to trade. The peace and order in the caliphate made it easier to transport goods from one side of the empire to the other. From Syria, for example, came steel and glassware; from Spain, there was leather. Goods were carried by caravans: convoys of fifty or more camels, which could survive on little food and water. Ships and caravans also brought goods from beyond the empire: in Baghdad's markets, you could buy spices and dyes from India; ivory and gold from Africa; silk and **ceramics** from China; and honey and slaves from Russia.

By law, different goods were sold in different areas. For example, in Baghdad, the Market of the Goldsmiths (*Sukh as-Sagah*) was near the main bridge over the River Tigris. This system helped customers to find what they needed, but it also gave them a fairer price, as in a street of rug sellers each trader had to compete in price with every other trader.

The potters of Baghdad were famed for the beautiful sheen they gave their ceramics, which included household items for cooking and serving food. Poorer people would have bought simple long-sleeved robes of wool or linen. Richer people could have purchased embroidered and vividly coloured cotton and silk robes, and decorated their homes with rugs, wall hangings and cushions. Metal items on sale were made from gold, silver, lead, brass, copper and iron. These expensive objects included tools, weapons and jewellery. Glassmakers sold jugs and delicate perfume bottles, patterned with coloured glasses or etched with designs.

In his book *Muqaddimah* ('Introduction'), the Muslim historian Ibn Khaldun (1332–1406 CE) said:

'When civilization increases… the customs and needs of luxury increase. Crafts are created to obtain luxury products.'

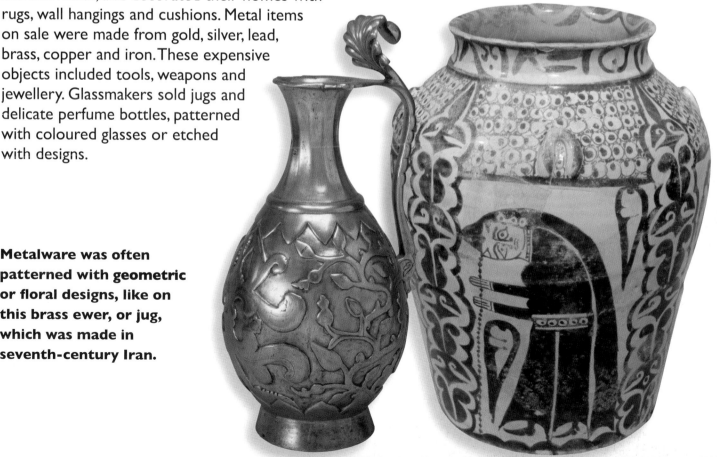

Earthenware pottery, strengthened by a hard, shiny glaze, was frequently used for household objects. This painted jug was made in tenth-century Iraq.

Metalware was often patterned with geometric or floral designs, like on this brass ewer, or jug, which was made in seventh-century Iran.

WHICH SPANISH CITY HAD THOUSANDS OF MOSQUES?

In 711 CE, under the orders of the Umayyad caliph al-Walid I, Muslim soldiers invaded the Iberian Peninsula and conquered most of modern-day Spain and Portugal. After seizing the city of Córdoba, the new Muslim rulers made it their capital.

Before the arrival of the Islamic army, most people on the Iberian Peninsula were Christians, alongside a fairly large population of Jews. Within a century, many people had converted to Islam. Even most of the remaining Christians were speaking Arabic. The Muslim rulers of Iberia called their lands al-Andalus. At first, al-Andalus was a province of the caliphate, ruled by the Umayyads from Damascus. Then, in 750 CE, the Umayyad dynasty was overthrown by the Abbasids. An Umayyad prince called Abd al-Rahman I (731–88 CE) fled from Damascus to al-Andalus. He established Umayyad rule over al-Andalus and broke away from the rest of the empire. In 784 CE, Abd al-Rahman I ordered the construction of the Great Mosque of Córdoba. It was to be the largest mosque ever seen in al-Andalus.

At the end of his life, Abd al-Rahman III (889–961 CE), ruler of al-Andalus, said:

'I have now reigned above fifty years... Riches and honours, power and pleasure, have waited on my call, nor does any earthly blessing appear to have been wanting to my felicity. In this situation, I have diligently numbered the days of pure and genuine happiness which have fallen to my lot: they amount to fourteen.'

What shape were the arches in Córdoba's Great Mosque?

The Great Mosque of Córdoba was constructed out of the ruins of a Christian church. In 1236 CE, during the Reconquista, it was converted back into a church.

By the early tenth century, Cordóba had grown into one of the world's largest cities, with around 500,000 inhabitants. The city boasted 3,000 mosques and 300 public baths, where people bathed and chatted, as was Arabic custom. In 961 CE, the Umayyad prince al-Hakam II inherited al-Andalus. Under his rule, Cordóba reached its peak as a centre of learning. Al-Hakam built up a huge library, which some people said contained 600,000 books. That would have made it the world's largest. He encouraged scientists, doctors, **translators** and writers to move to Cordóba from across the empire.

During the eleventh century, the Christian kingdoms of northern Spain started to conquer al-Andalus. This period is known as the Reconquista ('reconquest'). Cordóba was taken by the Christians in 1236 CE. Granada, the last Muslim city in Spain, fell to the Christians in 1492 CE. At first, Muslims lived quite peacefully under Christian rule, but over time Spain's rulers put pressure on Muslims to convert to Christianity. In 1501 CE, Spanish law offered the last remaining Muslims a choice: convert to Christianity or leave Spain.

The *mihrab* of Cordóba's Great Mosque is decorated by mosaics of plants and quotations from the Quran. A mihrab is a niche in the wall facing Mecca, towards which Muslims should pray.

The beautiful Alhambra in Granada was built as a palace fortress by the city's Muslim rulers. Its many pools and fountains symbolized the waters of Paradise.

DETECTIVE WORK

Explore the Alhambra palace for yourself on an interactive walking tour: http://www. saudiaramcoworld.com/ issue/200604/alhambra/.

WAS EDUCATION IMPORTANT?

Before the coming of Islam, most Arabs could not read or write. But Islam set great value on education, because it meant that people could read the Quran. During the golden age of Islamic civilization, many children went to school.

By the tenth century, most towns and villages had at least one *maktab*, or primary school. From the age of about six, children were taught reading, writing and Islamic studies. However, many poor children could not go to school, as they had to help their parents with their work. A woman's role in life was usually to be a mother, so although some girls did attend a maktab, very few stayed on after the age of twelve. Boys left the maktab in their mid- to late teens. Some boys — and, occasionally, some girls — went on to higher education, at a *madrasa*. Madrasas were usually part of a mosque. In the early days of the empire, madrasas taught only Islamic studies and law. Later, they taught whatever their teachers specialized in, from maths to music or medicine.

DETECTIVE WORK

Find out about the different styles of calligraphy used in the Islamic Empire by exploring the Bibliothèque Nationale de France's Arabic manuscripts: http://expositions.bnf.fr/livrarab/anglais/index.htm.

The oldest madrasa still in use today is the University of al-Karaouine in the city of Fes (in modern Morocco). It was founded in 859 CE by a wealthy female merchant called Fatima al-Fihri.

The first paper factory opened in Baghdad in 793 CE, using techniques learnt from the Chinese. Before they could use paper, writers had used papyrus (made from the papyrus plant), which was fragile, or parchment (made from animal skin), which was expensive. Now the easy production of paper led to a huge rise in the making and selling of books. Soon bookshops clustered around the main mosque of every city. Muslim scholars wrote about history and geography, as well as exciting stories such as the *One Thousand and One Nights* (often called *The Arabian Nights*), which was a collection of folk tales.

Public libraries were set up in major cities, with reading rooms open to everyone. Large libraries had their own **calligraphers** and book-binders. The most famous library of all was Baghdad's House of Wisdom (*Bayt al-Hikma*), which held 400,000 books. It was funded by the caliph al-Ma'mun (786–833 CE). Here he employed hundreds of people to translate books from across the world into Arabic, while scholars studied subjects from **astronomy** to **zoology**.

These scholars are holding a debate in a library. The illustration is from a twelfth-century book by the poet al-Hariri.

This thirteenth-century illustration shows a scribe (someone who copies books by hand) using a reed pen and ink.

🐾 **Which art form, practised by scribes, was among the most respected in the Islamic Empire?**

In 1377 CE, the historian Ibn Khaldun wrote in his *Muqaddimah*:

'*The sciences of… the Greeks, have come down to us, because they were translated through al-Ma'mun's efforts. He was successful in this direction because he had many translators at his disposal and spent much money in this connection.*'

WHO LOOKED AFTER THE POOR AND SICK?

Charity is at the heart of the Quran's teachings. The caliph's officials collected taxes from people across the empire. Some of that money was given to the poor, disabled, elderly, widows and orphans. The caliphs and other wealthy people paid for the building of hospitals, pharmacies, orphanages and soup kitchens, where the needy could be given food.

The caliph's government was split into offices, called *diwans*. The most important *diwans* were one that dealt with letter-writing and records, a second that collected taxes, and a third that paid expenses, such as to the poor. For several centuries after its birth in the seventh century, the Islamic Empire could be called the world's first welfare state. In a welfare state, the government tries to protect the health and wellbeing of its people. This is not to say that the poor and sick in the Islamic Empire were given the same standard of care as they might in wealthy countries today, but the caliphate was ahead of its time in its attempts to look after them.

The medical historian Ibn Abi Usaybi'ah (1203–70 CE) wrote about the al-Nuri hospital in Damascus:

'All patients were first examined in the external hall. Those who were not seriously ill were given medicines and sent home; those with more serious ailments were admitted to the hospital. They were bathed and given new clothes.'

The world's first pharmacies opened in Baghdad in late eighth century. In this thirteenth-century illustration, pharmacists can be seen making a medicine, surrounded by their jars of plants, herbs and chemicals.

A large hospital and mosque were built at Divrigi (in modern Turkey) in 1228–9 CE.

This illustration shows a patient having a growth on his neck removed by a surgeon. The patient is being restrained by the surgeon's assistant.

During the golden age of Islamic civilization, hospitals were built in most major cities, with a staff including surgeons, doctors and nurses. Separate wards often took care of the mentally ill. All hospitals required their doctors to hold diplomas from a respected medical school. By the tenth century, laws had been passed to keep hospitals open 24 hours a day and to stop them turning away patients who could not afford to pay.

The empire's doctors took huge steps forward in medicine, including gaining a better understanding of many diseases and how the body works. They wrote countless books, which were later translated into other languages and used as textbooks in Europe for centuries. For example, the doctor Ibn Masawaiyh (777–857 CE) wrote books on fevers, hygiene and the workings of the human eye.

Perhaps the most famous doctor of the Islamic Empire was al-Zahrawi (936–1013 CE), who lived in Córdoba. He is often called the father of modern surgery because of his breakthroughs. He was the first person to use forceps to pull out a baby during childbirth. He invented surgical instruments that are still used today, including an instrument for examining inside the ear.

Unluckily for people having painful operations in the early Islamic world, what had not yet been invented?

DETECTIVE WORK

You can discover some more facts about al-Zahrawi and his breakthroughs on the Science Museum's website: http://www.sciencemuseum.org.uk/broughttolife/people/albucasis.aspx.

WHAT DID ISLAMIC ASTRONOMERS DISCOVER?

Islamic scholars studied the scientific discoveries of the ancient Greeks, Persians and Indians, and then made discoveries of their own. Islamic astronomers made huge breakthroughs in our understanding of the movements of the planets. Most astronomers were also mathematicians. Many of the mathematical methods taught in our classrooms were developed in the Islamic Empire.

Several Abbasid caliphs, in particular the knowledge-loving al-Ma'mun, made it their business to fund the work of astronomers. Baghdad and Damascus became great centres for astronomical study. The world's first modern-style **observatory**, the Shammasiyah, was built in Baghdad in around 828 CE, during the reign of al-Ma'mun. In this and many other observatories across the civilization, careful measurements were made of the movements of the Sun, Moon and planets. Detailed maps of the stars were drawn.

In this illustration, Islamic astronomers, surrounded by their books, are demonstrating the use of a variety of instruments.

DETECTIVE WORK

Use the American Institute of Physics website to carry out some more research on the instruments used by early Islamic astronomers: http://www.aip.org. Type 'Naked Eyes' into the 'Search' box.

🐾 **Can you name an instrument used by early Islamic astronomers?**

In around 830 CE, a group of Baghdad astronomers worked out the **circumference** of the Earth as 39,900 km (24,792 miles), which is extraordinarily close to the actual distance of 40,075 km (24,901 miles). A few decades later, the Islamic astronomer al-Battani (858–929 CE) calculated the length of the solar year (the time it takes the Earth to travel once around the Sun): 365 days, 5 hours, 46 minutes and 24 seconds – just over 2 minutes out.

Ibn al-Haytham (c.965–1040 CE) was a mathematician and astronomer who is often described as the first true **physicist**. He made great strides in optics (the study of light), with his work on mirrors and lenses. One story tells us that he was ordered by the ruler of Egypt, al-Hakim, to use his skills to regulate the floods of the River Nile. Al-Haytham knew the task was impossible. To escape being sentenced to death by the disappointed ruler, he pretended to have lost his mind. Luckily for the scientist, after al-Hakim died in 1021 CE, he was able to prove his sanity and continue with his work.

The word 'algebra' comes from the work of mathematician al-Khwarizmi (c.780–850 CE). It is still used to describe a method of solving equations. In 830 CE, al-Khwarizmi wrote:

'That fondness for science... has encouraged me to compose a short work on calculating by al-jabr [algebra] and al-muqabala [balancing equations], confining it to what is easiest and most useful in arithmetic.'

▶ **In 964 CE, the astronomer al-Sufi published his *Book of the Fixed Stars*. Here the constellation of Andromeda is in red, marked on a drawing of Andromeda, a character from Greek myth.**

▼ **This illustration shows an eclipse of the Moon (when it passes into the Earth's shadow). It appeared in the works of the astronomer al-Biruni (973–1048 CE).**

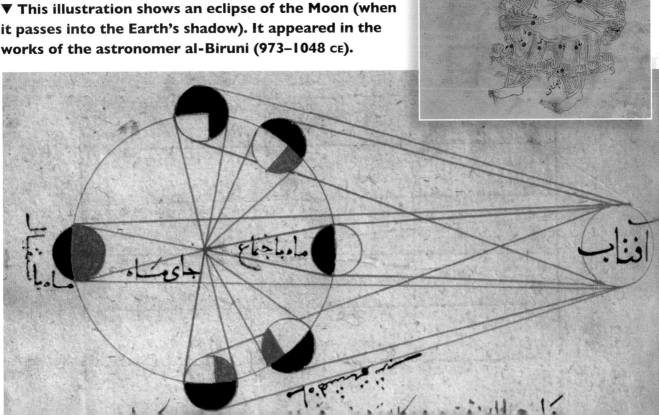

WHO INVENTED THE ELEPHANT CLOCK?

In 1136 CE, a man known as al-Jazari was born in southeastern Turkey. His father was chief engineer to the local Muslim ruler. When al-Jazari grew up, he took over from his father as engineer and went on to become one of the greatest inventors in the Islamic world. One of his inventions was an amazing elephant clock.

Al-Jazari is most famous today for the book he completed in 1206 CE, which is known in English as the *Book of Knowledge of Mechanical Devices*. The book is rather like a do-it-yourself manual. In it, al-Jazari described and drew 50 inventions, in such detail that they could be built by a skilled reader. None of al-Jazari's own constructions have survived, but modern engineers have built some of his devices – and they work. The book contains designs for clocks, fountains, water pumps and automata (machines or robots that were moved by systems of wheels, pulleys and balls). One of the clocks in the book was a water clock in the shape of an elephant.

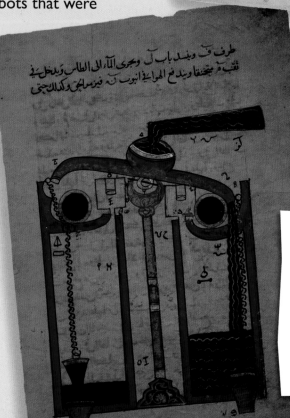

Al-Jazari built his machines, such as this water-raising device, by trial and error. If a system did not work, he tried something else.

This drawing of al-Jazari's elephant clock is labelled to show its parts. Every half-hour, a system of strings made the elephant driver pound his drum to announce the time.

DETECTIVE WORK

Find out exactly how al-Jazari's elephant clock worked by watching this video: http://www.1001inventions.com/media/video/clock.

Water clocks first appeared in ancient Egypt and Babylon, from around 1600 BCE. These used a steady flow of water into or out of a container, where the level of water could be measured to estimate time. Inside al-Jazari's elephant clock was a water-filled bucket with a bowl floating in it. The bowl had a hole in it, through which it filled with water every half-hour, making it sink. As it sank, the bowl pulled a string that released a ball, which dropped into the mouth of a snake. The snake tilted, lifting the bowl out of the water so the process could start again.

Many of al-Jazari's inventions were probably just intended to amuse his employer. Among these were automata such as his drink-serving robot waitress and musical robot band. Simple automata had been built centuries before al-Jazari, but his inventions took great leaps forward. His use of rolling balls, which sounded the hours on drums and moved machinery, can be seen in some modern toys.

Many people in early Islamic civilization still had to collect their water from wells and rivers. As chief engineer, al-Jazari's designs for water pumps and supply systems were put to vital practical use. He was the first to use gears to create a water supply system driven by a waterwheel and pump. It carried water from the river uphill through pipes to the city of Diyarbakir (in modern Turkey).

One of al-Jazari's inventions was a boat that moved across the water by itself. He wrote:

'The boat is placed on the surface of a large pool of water, and is seldom stationary but moves in the surface of the water. All the time it moves the sailors move, because they are on axles, and the oars move it through the water until about half-an-hour has elapsed.'

The castle water clock did a lot more than just tell the time: the five robotic musicians played a tune whenever a lever was pulled, while the two birds dropped balls into vases.

🐾 **Al-Jazari's castle water clock charted the movements of which star constellations across the sky?**

WHERE DID ISLAMIC EXPLORERS TRAVEL?

With their convoys of camels, Islamic merchants travelled across the empire and beyond, into central Africa and China. By sea, their ships traded with Europe, Africa, India and Southeast Asia. Some Muslim travellers, such as the famous al-Masudi, were not driven by trade but by the fascination of exploration itself.

Many Muslim scholars studied the geography of the empire, and some travelled far beyond it. Their travels were made safer by the well-used trade routes across land and ocean. Merchants and explorers sailed across the seas on ships that we call dhows. These sturdy ships had lateen (almost triangular) sails, which coped well with the sudden storms of the Indian Ocean. Few Muslim travellers journeyed far without an astrolabe to help with navigation. An astrolabe is an instrument that is used to work out latitude (the distance north or south of the equator). Although astrolabes were invented by the ancient Greeks, Islamic scientists made them more exact.

DETECTIVE WORK

Research the boats, routes and stories of Islamic seafaring on the Mariners' Museum website: http://ageofex.marinersmuseum.org. Click on 'The Explorers' and then 'Arab Exploration'.

This thirteenth-century illustration shows a typical Arab dhow, which is pointed at both bow (front) and stern (back).

🐾 **What material were dhows built with?**

One of the most famous Islamic explorers was al-Masudi (c.896–956 CE), who travelled to eastern Africa, China, India and Sri Lanka. In his book *The Meadows of Gold and Mines of Gems*, he wrote about the seas he sailed on, their waterspouts, whales and fishes; the customs and trades he came across, from pearl fishing to Hindu funerals; and the personalities of the rulers, merchants and slaves he heard of and met with.

Islamic map-makers combined the maps made by earlier civilizations with the information they received from Muslim explorers and merchants. The most renowned of these map-makers was al-Idrisi (1099–1165/6 CE). He travelled through parts of Europe and western Asia, and even visited York in England. In 1154 CE, while in the employment of Roger II, King of Sicily, he completed his groundbreaking map book, often called the *Tabula Rogeriana* (after his employer). It was the most accurate world map ever drawn and would remain the most accurate for the next 300 years.

In his book *The Meadows of Gold and Mines of Gems*, al-Masudi wrote:

'The author of this work compares himself to a man, who having found pearls of all kinds and colours, gathers them together into a necklace and makes them into an ornament that its possessor guards with great care. My aim has been to trace the lands and the histories of many peoples, and I have no other.'

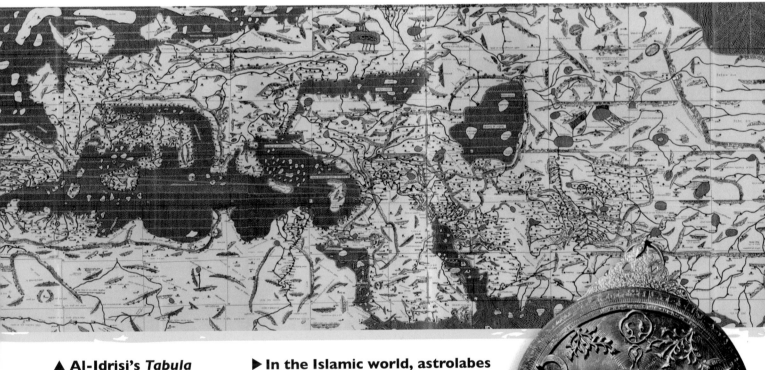

▲ Al-Idrisi's *Tabula Rogeriana* contained maps of Europe, Asia and North Africa. This modern copy is a combination of several maps in the book.

▶ In the Islamic world, astrolabes were used not only for navigation but also for time-keeping, astronomy and finding the direction of Mecca for prayer. This brass astrolabe was made in Cairo in 1236 CE.

YOUR PROJECT

Now you have learnt about the history of Islamic civilization, you are ready to put together your own project. Perhaps you could concentrate on the subject that interests you most of all. Maybe it will be warriors and their weapons, al-Jazari and his inventions, or the story of Baghdad.

A great idea for a project is to choose an Islamic object, whether it's a sword or a jug, and write its story. Perhaps you could find your object in a museum, or on a museum website. Who made your object? Where was it sold? Another idea for a project is to choose two mosques, one ancient and one modern, and compare them. Perhaps your ancient mosque could be the Great Mosque of Kairouan, in Tunisia, and your modern one could be the Hassan II Mosque in Casablanca, Morocco. You will find lots of websites about them. Why do you think the mosques are similar? If some features are different, why do you think that is?

How about pretending you are a time-travelling journalist who has to interview a great character from early Islamic civilization? Will you choose a caliph, such as science-loving al-Ma'mun, or a groundbreaking doctor, like al-Zahrawi? What questions will you ask? If you were really interested by the markets, storytellers and racecourses of Baghdad, here is one last project idea. Imagine you are taking a walk through Baghdad in the ninth or tenth century. Where do you go? Whom do you meet?

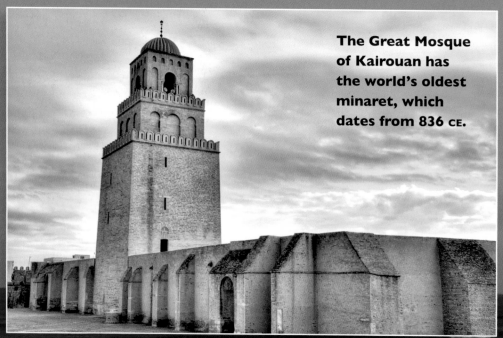

The Great Mosque of Kairouan has the world's oldest minaret, which dates from 836 CE.

Project presentation

● First of all, research your project really carefully. Visit your local library and the school library to find books about your subject. Try to take a tour of your local mosque or a museum with a collection of Islamic objects.

● You will find a wealth of information about Islamic civilization on the Internet. Put together a list of useful websites: include museum websites, websites for mosques and palaces, and some that include stories about great cities and famous characters.

● To illustrate your project, print out pictures of Islamic objects and buildings that you find on the Internet. Buy postcards from the museums you visit. You could also do drawings of your local mosque or of Islamic art that you find on websites.

The Hassan II Mosque, which was completed in 1993, stands right on the edge of the Atlantic Ocean. It boasts the tallest minaret in the world: 210 m (689 ft) high.

You could base your project on this jug, which was made in the tenth or eleventh century by a potter who worked in the region of modern Iran.

GLOSSARY

ﷺ Arabic for 'peace be upon him'. It is respectful to say this after using the name of the Prophet Muhammad.

Abbasids A family who ruled the Islamic Empire 750–1258 CE.

Arabic The language of Arabia, in the Middle East.

astrologers People who study the movements of stars and planets and their supposed effect on humans.

astronomy Study of the stars and planets.

BCE 'Before the Common Era'. Used to signify dates before the birth of Jesus.

caliphate An area ruled by a caliph, the chief Muslim religious and political leader.

calligraphers People who practise the art of beautiful handwriting.

CE 'Common Era'. Used to signify dates since the birth of Jesus.

ceramics Products made from baked clay.

chainmail Armour made from linked metal rings.

circumference Distance round the outside of a circle or sphere.

converting Causing someone to change their religious beliefs.

dynasty A ruling family.

empire Group of countries under the rule of one leader.

geometric With regular, repeating lines or shapes.

golden age A time of great developments in the sciences and arts.

irrigation Watering of fields by channelling water along ditches and canals.

Middle East Region covering modern countries from Egypt in the west to Iran in the east.

mosaics Patterns made from small pieces of coloured glass or stone.

navy A country or state's war ships and crews.

observatory A building equipped for the study of the stars and planets.

pagans People who worship many gods.

physicist A person who studies the behaviour of matter and energy.

provinces Areas of an empire or country that are distant from its capital.

Ramadan Ninth month of the Muslim year, when Muslims fast.

rebel A person who fights against the government.

revelation A communication from God.

skirmishes Short bursts of fighting.

symbolize To be a symbol, or sign, of.

taxes Money demanded from the people by a government.

translators People who change books from one language to another.

Umayyad A family who ruled the Islamic Empire 661–750 CE.

zoology Study of animals.

Zoroastrians People who follow the teachings of Zoroaster, who lived in Iran 3,500–4,000 years ago.

ANSWERS

Page 5   The dome is topped by a copper full-moon shape, which faces towards Mecca. Many Islamic states have used a crescent moon as their symbol.

Page 7   It signalled a mosque's location, and the call to prayer, or *adhan*, was made from its top.

Page 9   Lances were used to knock opponents off their horses or camels.

Page 11   Mosque courtyards had several uses: they were where worshippers washed before praying, they were meeting places, and they kept adjoining rooms cool in a hot climate.

Page 12   Baghdad was next to the River Tigris and close to the River Euphrates, with man-made canals linking the two. These provided water for the city and transport for goods.

Page 14   Musicians often played a stringed, guitar-like instrument called an *oud*.

Page 16   Horseshoe arches (round arches which widen before rounding off) were used.

Page 19   Calligraphy was highly respected. Before the invention of printing, it was the only way of preserving the Quran and spreading knowledge.

Page 21   A safe general anaesthetic (causing loss of consciousness) had not yet been invented.

Page 22   The astronomers in the illustration are using a sextant and quadrant (for measuring the angle between a planet or star and the horizon), an astrolabe (for locating the positions of the planets) and an hourglass (for measuring time).

Page 25   It charted the movements of the zodiac constellations (seen on the dial at the top).

Page 26   Dhows were made from wooden planks, stitched together with rope.

FURTHER INFORMATION

Books to read

The History and Activities of the Islamic Empire by Gary Barr (Heinemann Library, 2007)

Islam (Eyewitness) by Philip Wilkinson (Dorling Kindersley, 2002)

Islam (Religion in Focus) by Geoff Teece (Franklin Watts, 2008)

Websites

http://www.bbc.co.uk/religion/religions/islam/

http://www.britishmuseum.org/explore/cultures/middle_east/islamic_middle_east.aspx

http://www.vam.ac.uk/page/i/islamic-middle-east/

Note to parents and teachers: Every effort has been made by the publishers to ensure that these websites are suitable for children. However, because of the nature of the Internet, it is impossible to guarantee that the contents of these sites will not be altered. We strongly advise that Internet access is supervised by a responsible adult.

Places to visit

Birmingham Central Mosque, Birmingham, B12 0XS

British Museum, London, WC1B 3DG

Islamic Cultural Centre, London, NW8 7RG

Swansea Mosque, Swansea, SA1 4AW

Victoria and Albert Museum, London, SW7 2RL

INDEX

Numbers in **bold** refer to pictures and captions.